I'm Going To READ!™

These levels are meant only as guides;
you and your child can best choose a book that's right.

Level 1: Kindergarten–Grade 1 . . . Ages 4–6

- word bank to highlight new words
- consistent placement of text to promote readability
- easy words and phrases
- simple sentences build to make simple stories
- art and design help new readers decode text

UP TO
50
WORDS

Level 2: Grade 1 . . . Ages 6–7

- word bank to highlight new words
- rhyming texts introduced
- more difficult words, but vocabulary is still limited
- longer sentences and longer stories
- designed for easy readability

UP TO
100
WORDS

Level 3: Grade 2 . . . Ages 7–8

- richer vocabulary of up to 200 different words
- varied sentence structure
- high-interest stories with longer plots
- designed to promote independent reading

UP TO
200
WORDS

Level 4: Grades 3 and up . . . Ages 8 and up

- richer vocabulary of more than 300 different words
- short chapters, multiple stories, or poems
- more complex plots for the newly independent reader
- emphasis on reading for meaning

MORE THAN
300
WORDS

LEVEL 2

Library of Congress Cataloging-in-Publication Data Available

2 4 6 8 10 9 7 5 3 1

Published by Sterling Publishing Co., Inc.
387 Park Avenue South, New York, NY 10016
Text copyright © 2005 by Harriet Ziefert Inc.
Illustrations copyright © 2005 by Tanya Roitman
Distributed in Canada by Sterling Publishing
c/o Canadian Manda Group, 165 Dufferin Street
Toronto, Ontario, Canada M6K 3H6
Distributed in Great Britain and Europe by Chris Lloyd at Orca Book
Services, Stanley House, Fleets Lane, Poole BH15 3AJ, England
Distributed in Australia by Capricorn Link (Australia) Pty. Ltd.
P.O. Box 704, Windsor, NSW 2756, Australia

I'm Going To Read is a trademark of Sterling Publishing Co., Inc.

Sterling ISBN 1-4027-2076-9

I'm Going To
READ!
TM

I'm Going to New York to Visit the Lions

Pictures by Tanya Roitman

Sterling Publishing Co., Inc.
New York

My name is Nate.
I'm going to New York.

I'm going to New York
to visit the lions.

My friend is Kate.

I tell her where I'm going.

"I'm going to visit the lions."

Kate asks, "What lions?"

"Are you going to visit
the lions in the zoo?"

not   way

"No way, Kate.
Not those lions!"

Then Kate asks, "Are you going to visit the lions at the museum?"

I answer, "No way, Kate.
Not stuffed lions."

Then Kate asks, "Are you going to visit the lions at a toy store?"

toy

"No way, Kate.
Not toy lions!"

"I'm going to visit the lions
at the library."

"What library?" asks Kate.

"I am visiting the lions at

the New York Public Library!"

"Nate, what does it
say up there?"

"It says: Patience.
Patience and Fortitude guard
the entrance to the library."

"Come on, Kate. Let's walk
between the lions and go inside."

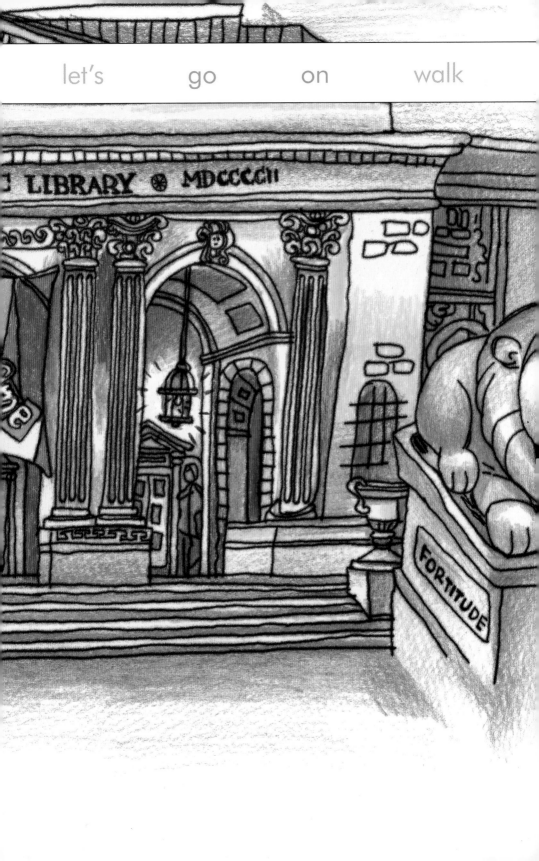

"Nate, where are the books?"

"The books are not here.
The books are downstairs."

"Upstairs there is a very big
reading room."

"People read the books in this library.
They take notes."

"But they cannot
take the books home."

"More than one million books live
at the New York Public Library.
And so do the lions!"